......

Published by
Extra MILE Innovators
54 Montgomery Avenue, Kingston 10, Jamaica W.I.
www.extramileja.com
ruthtaylor@extramileja.com

Edited by: Carlene Dacres
Cover Designed by: Christopher Lawrence and Amoy A. Lawrence,
The Anointed Writer

AUTHOR CONTACT

For Conferences, Workshops, Crusades, Conventions, Seminars,
Youth Ministry Development Consultation Contact: Erraldo L.
Budhan. Email elbministry@gmail.com| Tel: 876-803-4626.

30 Days of Encouragement

POWER

UP

Faith. Hope. Trust (Vol. 1)

ERRALDO L. BUDHAN

Extra MILE Innovators
Kingston, Jamaica W.I.

NOTES

DEDICATION

To my young brothers D'Jean and ReJean Budhan
For whom I try my very best to be an inspiration and a
role model.

ENDORSEMENTS

Victoria Osteen said, "As you keep your mind and heart focused in the right direction, approaching each day with faith and gratitude, I believe you will be empowered to live life to the fullest and enjoy the abundant life He (God) has promised you." After reading the book *Power Up,* I truly understand the quote of Victoria Osteen. I have truly been blessed by the encouraging words and practical examples laid out in the testimonials. This not just a devotional but it is a book that causes you to do introspection to see where you are in life and where you want to be.

Faith, hope and trust are not just built by reading but they are built by applying what you have read and depending on God totally. This devotional, though simple, has made a tremendous impact on my life in terms of building up those three vital components needed in my Christian journey. Conducting a daily devotional during any stage of a person's Christian life is one that takes discipline. This book makes it feel less of a chore and more of a privilege to grow in the faith. At whatever stage we are in our Christian life, we all at some point will need to sit back, take ourselves away from the pressures of the world and **Power Up.**

Power Up so that you can handle the task ahead and build a stronger relationship with the creator. I fully endorse this book especially to young adults who are always on the move. This book is compact and can be taken anywhere and the daily devotionals are of reasonable length that will impact your life greatly. Power Up and be great.

Ms. Shanice Senior
Bsc. Psychology (minor in Anthropology)
Administrative Assistant

*****

Every believer should seek to live a life of power or *Dunamis* as the Greek language would put it. Our heavenly Father wants us to practice the ways of the kingdom and living in the power of the Lord is the way to go. Jesus is the essential figure of such a lifestyle therefore, as Christians we should crave and embrace that reality.

In a world where Christianity is under both physical and spiritual attack, there is a great need for another material like the book, *Power Up,* by Erraldo. The author has skilfully projected the plan of God for our daily lives in a timely manner to reach and teach the principles of Kingdom power.

This life-changing devotional has the ability to encourage the fainting heart, and empower the Devoted. I endorse this material and encourage everyone to get into the habit of powering up.

Minister Leroy Hutchinson
Author & National Youth Director for C.O.G.O.P
Jamaica, Managing Director for Operation
Youth REAP Ltd.

*****

If your faith has grown a little weak, this devotional will renew and recharge it. Erraldo Budhan's undoubtedly God-directed life is an inspiration and will reassure readers that God has a purpose for all of us. It reaffirms my belief that everything happens for a reason and carries with it a lesson to mature us. I love the fact that at the end of each chapter there's an activity specifically designed to lift the faith of the reader. I can't wait to see what this inspiring author comes up with next. It is a fascinating read!

Carlene Dacres
Guidance Counsellor

ACKNOWLEDGMENTS

I thank God for the knowledge, wisdom and persistence in completing this book. I also want to thank my good friend Camille Webber for always encouraging me to write until completed. My family plays an integral role in my life and has contributed greatly to my growth and development. I want to extend love and blessings to my parents, Murphy and Raffie Budhan, and my grandmother Grace Bromfield for always reminding me how proud they are of me.

Thank you to my editor Carlene Dacres and my proofreaders: Amanda Cooke, Shanice Senior and Richard Robinson for ensuring the book is error free.

Thanks to you, readers for taking the time out to purchase and read this book.

INTRODUCTION

I beseech you therefore, brethren, by the mercies of God, that ye present your bodies a living sacrifice, holy, acceptable unto God, which is your reasonable service (Romans 12:1 KJV).

By the grace of God, this book was written to encourage you, a believer in Christ, to be the best you can be in Him. A companion guide means you take it everywhere you go along with your bible and read the daily encouragements offered. This book blossomed out of inspiring friends on Facebook by sharing a thoughtful message each day as a means of encouraging those who would read it to stay focused on the things that God has for them and the plans God has for them to complete.

The *Power Up Series* **is designed to build your trust, faith and hope in God.** Each volume in the series has an encouraging word for 30 days out of the 365 days of the year. The encouraging words are explained and a Bible verse is given. In Volume 1, you are reminded that you are here for a purpose and this book is designed to encourage you to never give up, and help you to fulfil that purpose.

There are other books are out there that are designed with this concept in mind. However, In *Power Up,* every text comes with testimony as well as an explanation made applicable to this contemporary era. You will be able to apply each encouragement and text to your life, watch God work and see your faith grow. Each encouragement carries a reflection. The reflection is to see the encouragement activated in your life.

After the reflection, you are encouraged to write a declaration in the book for each day. Declare that, "**By the mercies of God I will be GREAT or I will PRAY MORE."** Whatever it is that you need from God, declare that you will have it. You will write the declaration as a prayer to God. Whatever you need to do to be the best you, and see the will of God working in your life, declare you shall be that person.

Each day you will be encouraged to do great, be great, experience great things and reflect on the greatness of Jehovah God.

I beseech you therefore, brethren, by the mercies of God: READ AND BE GREAT!

TABLE OF CONTENTS

Day 1

ASK GOD FOR THE BIG THINGS

Matthew 7:7-11 is a strong encouragement to us to ASK God all that we want Him to do for, in and through us.

Ask, and it will be given to you; seek, and you will find; knock, and it will be opened to you. For everyone who asks receives, and he who seeks finds, and to him who knocks it will be opened. Or what man is there among you who, when his son asks for a loaf, will give him a stone? Or if he asks for a fish, he will not give him a snake, will he? If you then, being evil, know how to give good gifts to your children, how much more will your Father who is in

1

heaven give what is good to those who ask Him! *(Matthew 7:7-11, NIV)*

Encouragement

We are encouraged to ask God for whatever we want and He promised us that we shall receive it. Asking is simple. All you need to do is express your heart to God with simple words. You do not need to speak in tongues or even in Standard English. Speak the language that you are comfortable with. Growing up, I thought I must pray to God in the King James Version of the Bible. I thought God did not understand the Jamaican language until I realized that God created languages and he speaks every language, broken or standard. After coming to that realization, I began to pray in my heart language and I asked God for everything I needed. I was encouraged to go to God in prayer and I realized prayer works. Do not think to yourself that you are not praying right or you are not using the right words. When you are talking to God, just talk. Ask Him what you may and pose to Him all the hard questions and all the big dreams for He says in His word that if you ASK, you will receive.

Testimony

I had just completed my Bachelor of Arts degree in Theology with a minor in Guidance and Counselling, and I asked the Lord to open a door for me. I told God that I didn't want to be like others who studied and took months to get a job. I prayed and as simple as the prayer may be, I got a job a month before I graduated. It wasn't the desired job that I wanted, but it was a job nonetheless. I then started to pray specifically. There are times when you pray broadly but there are times when you must be specific. I was in a job that I was not able to use my degree to impact lives so I resigned from the job in July. I prayed to God at that same time and said: "Lord I need a job as a Guidance Counsellor." September came and I got no call. I went back to God and prayed again.

Never think that you are annoying God by repetitive prayer. Pray the same thing over and over because God can never get annoyed by hearing from you. One Monday in mid-September, I got a job interview as a Guidance Counsellor. On the Tuesday, I was confirmed as the new Guidance Counsellor and by the Wednesday, I started working as the only male Guidance Counsellor in a Kingston-based high school for eight months.

I beseech you therefore, brethren, by the mercies of God: Ask God for the big things.

The things that you think seem impossible are very much possible in the eyes of God. Asking comes with faith. Never stop asking God for the things you want. If it is in His will, He will grant it to you.

Brawta Scripture

"Now to Him who is able to do immeasurably more than all we **ask** or **imagine**, according to His power that is at work within us" (Ephesians 3:20, NIV).

REFLECTION

What do you want God to do for you?

_____

_____

_____

_____

_____

_____

Prayer

I encourage you to ask. Let's pray:

> "Father, we ask of you to give us, through your son Jesus Christ, the faith to ask you for everything that we need. This we pray through the power of your Holy Spirit." Amen.

Write to God

_____

_____

_____

_____

_____

_____

_____

_____

_____

_____

_____

_____

_____

Day 2

DO NOT BE ANXIOUS

The verse below in Philippians encourages us that when we ask God for things, we must be patient, not anxious.

"Do not be anxious about anything, but in every situation, by prayer and petition, with thanksgiving, present your requests to God" (Philippians 4:6, NIV).

Encouragement

We are encouraged to not live in anxiety. People who struggle with anxiety oftentimes worry a lot. Why worry when you can pray? Scripture assures you and me that we must not be uneasy, nervous, fearful of anything but in all things, in every situation we are faced with in life, we must pray and make our petition known to God. Today you are encouraged to ask God to remove anxiety or any other thing that may be holding you down from seeing His promises being fulfilled in your life. What did you ask God for in the previous reading? Are you struggling to believe it will happen? Why worry? God has the answer to all your questions. Be anxious for nothing but in everything make your request known unto God and He will respond to you.

Testimony

I tried everything in my powers to get a car. Every time I thought I would get the breakthrough so I could stop renting vehicles, the breakthrough fell through. I almost gave up on this car idea. I prayed and asked God again, "Please make the process smoother for me to get a vehicle." After submitting certain documents to the bank, I started to become anxious. I was worried about them denying my application for a loan and I worried for almost one week. Anxiety was my bread, day and night until my mother shared something with me. She said: "Why worry, if it is God's will for you to get it then you will get it, just pray." Those wise words calmed my spirit and I began to ask the Lord again for a favour but before I did that, I made sure I prayed against the spirit of doubt and anxiety. One week before going to Mexico to do missions, the bank called me and told me that my loan was confirmed and I could pick up the vehicle and drive home. Why worry when you can pray?

I beseech you therefore, brethren, by the mercies of God:

Pray more. Worry less. Whenever you pray, ask God to remove the spirit of doubt, fear and anxiety. Whenever you feel anxious, remember that anxiety is not of God. Be bold and trust God. When you feel anxious, pray more and make your request known unto God and He will respond.

Brawta Scripture

"Cast your cares on the Lord and He will sustain you; He will never let the righteous be shaken" (Psalm 55:22, NIV).

REFLECTION

What are you anxious about?

_____

_____

_____

_____

_____

_____

_____

_____

_____

_____

Prayer

I encourage you to pray more and worry less. Let's pray:

> Father, we ask of you to give us, through your son Jesus Christ, the strength to pray more and worry less about the simple things. Remind us that you hold the future in your hands and that our lives are controlled by you. This we pray through the power of your Holy Spirit. Amen.

What are you worrying about? Write them down and pray about them. PRAY MORE. WORRY LESS.

Write your request to God below:

_____

_____

_____

_____

_____

_____

_____

Day 3

DO NOT GIVE UP!

We are encouraged in the text below to never give up.

"But as for you, be strong and do not give up, for your work will be rewarded" (2 Chronicles 15:7, NIV).

Encouragement

Giving up is very easy. All you need to do is stop trying. But giving up is not an option. Life may seem rough and challenging but that is never a reason to give up on yourself or your goals. Also, never give up on people. Be strong. In the season where you feel you are at your weakest point BE STRONG. It sounds cliché and even questionable. How can one be strong when they are weak? Sometimes we experience weakness in our mind, spirit and our body. Being weak at times is normal but it's never an excuse to give up. In our weak times: be it weak in the mind, spirit or in our physical body be reminded that God's strength is made perfect in weakness. So, in the strength of the Lord be strong and never give up!

Testimony

I love preaching and I know I am called to that task for the Lord, but at a point on the Christian journey, I felt like giving up. I became weak spiritually, physically, mentally and even emotionally. I felt like giving up and just being a normal church member without certain responsibilities. Then I preached a sermon entitled "What happens when you cannot find God?" The sermon touched me and answered certain questions I had for God. At the end of the church service, someone came to me and said: "I am praying for you, do not stop what you are doing. The word you preached was a timely one for me." After hearing that I was convinced that giving up was not of God. I decided that I would never stop fulfilling my purpose. Even when life looks bleak, I'll be strong and never give up for my work will be rewarded.

I beseech you therefore, brethren, by the mercies of God: DO NOT GIVE UP.

Everything will not happen the way you want them to. Some things will happen in your life that may be hard for you to explain but let nothing stop you from completing the task you have to do. Let nothing and no one hinder you from fulfilling your purpose in God. Never give up because giving up is not for winners and you are in Christ MORE THAN CONQUEROR. You have what it takes to finish the race. Never give up because greatness is in you.

Brawta Scripture

"However, I consider my life worth nothing to me; my only aim is to finish the race and complete the task the Lord Jesus has given me--the task of testifying to the good news of God's grace" (Acts 20:24, NIV).

REFLECTION

What important things are you trying to accomplish or what important task are you trying to finish but feel frustrated and feel as if you want to give up?

_____

_____

_____

_____

_____

Write to God

_____

_____

_____

_____

Day 4

DO NOT BOW TO EVIL

We are encouraged in the text below never to bow to evil.

Shadrach, Meshach, and Abednego replied, O Nebuchadnezzar, we do not need to defend ourselves before you. If we are thrown into the blazing furnace, the God whom we serve is able to save us. He will rescue us from your power, Your Majesty. But even if he doesn't, we want to make it clear to you, Your Majesty, that we will never serve your gods or worship the gold statue you have set up (Daniel 3:16-18, NLT).

Encouragement

If we are true to ourselves, we will admit that there are times when evil presents itself to us in all shapes, forms and sizes. Though evil comes and for some, it looks tantalizing as we see in the book of Genesis with Adam and Eve eating the forbidden fruit, for others, it is like the three Hebrew boys. Daniel 3 speaks of a King called Nebuchadnezzar who had created an image of gold and had given detailed instructions relating to when those in Babylon must bow down and worship the image. Can you see in your life which idol is trying to take the place of God? Based on previous texts in the Bible, God does not give us consent to worship or bow to any other gods but Him.

Shadrach, Meshach and Abednego had some privilege given to them but there were some people in the province who did not like the three Hebrew boys so they told the King that the boys would not bow to the idol when directed to do so. The King summoned the boys who stood their ground and told the king that they would not bow. Out of fury, King Nebuchadnezzar threw them into a blazing furnace because of their decision never to bow to a created image. Just like the three Hebrew boys, we must be firm in our stance to tell the devil *I will not bow.* On Day 5, we will talk more on the furnace experience.

Testimony

All of us at some point in life must have gone through temptations that put us in a position to bow to evil or walk away from evil. For some of us, we bowed and repented and for others, we just walked away from evil. Not everyone is initially strong like the three Hebrew boys but the good thing about God is that He will forgive us if we repent genuinely.

I was placed in a position to lie. My cousins and I borrowed a car and drove out of our city. Neither of us had a license. We took turns driving and one of my cousins took the wheel and put the car into reverse. Upon reversing we ran into the back of a car that was owned by a police officer. We all ran out quickly and another cousin moved the car and we said we were going to drive away and act as if nothing happened. We had the plan but someone who was not saved encouraged us not to do so because it was not right.

After that, we all went to the person who owned the vehicle and pleaded guilty. We could have lied our way out and drove back to our house as if nothing happened but that would be us bowing to evil. Today, I have learnt to be responsible and if I'm at fault for something, instead of bowing to evil and lie, I would rather speak the truth for the sake of Christ.

I beseech you therefore, brethren, by the mercies of God: Do not bow to evil.

It may be that you are not in a position where you will have to lie your way out of, but maybe you are doing something else that is displeasing to God. What idol do you have in your life that is causing you to bow? Do not let evil cause you to stray from God. Be like the Hebrew boys and tell the Nebuchadnezzar in your life *I will not bow.*

Brawta Scripture

"Stay away from every kind of evil" (1 Thessalonians 5:22).

REFLECTION

What temptations do you need to overcome?

_____

_____

_____

_____

_____

_____

What idols do you have in your life that you need to destroy?

_____

_____

_____

_____

_____

Ask him to keep you from bowing to those idols and temptations.

Day 5

TRUST GOD IN THE FIRES OF LIFE

The text below encourages us that God is with us in our rough times; even in our fiery furnace.

But suddenly, Nebuchadnezzar jumped up in amazement and exclaimed to his advisers, "Didn't we tie up three men and throw them into the furnace?" "Yes, Your Majesty, we certainly did," they replied. "Look!" Nebuchadnezzar shouted. "I see four men, unbound, walking around in the fire unharmed! And the fourth looks like a god! (Daniel 3:24-25, NLT)

Encouragement

You can admit that sometimes life seems difficult. It is not always "Cloud 9" living. Sometimes you feel like you are in a furnace. The pressures of life seem to be burning you on all angles and truly if you think about it long and hard, you could have been consumed by those pressures if God was not by your side. Below will be the testimony of the three Hebrew boys.

Testimony

Three boys by the name Shadrach, Meshach and Abednego were faithful servants of Jehovah. Just like you and me, they had a passion for the Lord and the things concerning the Lord. They never expected to be in a precarious situation such as being thrown in a furnace but their decision to serve the Lord placed them in hot water; worse yet, a furnace that was lit seven times hotter than normal.

After being thrown in the furnace the Bible said that these Hebrew boys were walking around as if they were on a sandy beach playing hopscotch. The reason they were not consumed by the fire was that God was with them. They did not have on any high tech protective gear that would keep them alive, all they had was God; the best protection ever. In the fire, they were walking around and the king saw four men instead of three and was amazed to a point that he had to release the three Hebrew boys. On Day 6, I will share with you, from the same story of the three Hebrew boys, why you must live a life pleasing unto God.

I beseech you therefore, brethren, by the mercies of God: Trust God in the fires of life.

Life is not easy but, in every furnace you find yourselves, I can assure you that God is there with you and God will make sure you come out of the furnace alive and not even smelling like smoke. You have to trust God in the worst of times just as how you trust Him in the best of times. Let God take you through the fire for if He guides you, you will never be burnt.

Brawta Scripture

"Teach these new disciples to obey all the commands I have given you. And be sure of this: I am with you always, even to the end of the age"(Matthew 28:20, NLT).

REFLECTION

What are some of the fires that you are facing in life today?

_____

_____

_____

_____

_____

_____

_____

What furnace are you currently in?

_____

_____

_____

_____

_____

_____

I implore you to trust God and watch Him take you out smoke-free, burnt-free and looking brand new. Tell God the furnace you are in and ask Him to keep you safe until that season is over.

Write to God

_____

_____

_____

_____

_____

_____

_____

_____

_____

Day 6

LIVE A LIFE THAT CAN ENCOURAGE OTHERS TO SERVE GOD

The text below encourages us to live a life that can transform the lives of others.

Then Nebuchadnezzar came as close as he could to the door of the flaming furnace and shouted: 'Shadrach, Meshach, and Abednego, servants of the Most High God, come out! Come here!' (Daniel 3:26, NIV)

Encouragement

There is this beautiful song written by The Consolers entitled "May the Work I've Done Speak for Me." In that song, they penned the lyrics *May the life I live speak for me*. Your life must be able to say to someone **God is powerful** without you actually saying it. I have learnt that actions speak louder than words. No matter how good your vocabulary is, it's your actions that are always the loudest and most memorable. Your life is much louder and can be heard by everyone that looks at you.

We are encouraged through the text above to live a life that is pleasing to God. Nebuchadnezzar threw the three Hebrew boys into the fire but because of their faithfulness to God in the initial stage, and God's hand upon their lives, they were not burned. That sparked something in Nebuchadnezzar that he might have said to himself *their God must be real.* And so he hurried them out of the fire and started offering praise unto Jehovah God. Is your life encouraging others to serve the God you claim you are serving?

We have just completed the story of Nebuchadnezzar and the three Hebrew boys. I encourage you to read the story in its entirety. On Day 7, we start the journey of serving. We will take three days to be encouraged on serving the Lord in ministry.

Testimony

In 2011, I went to study Commercial Food Preparation at Heart Trust/NTA. I did a Level 1 and 2 Studies in the space of 10 months, and during my time there I did not realize that I was being watched. I laugh really loud and I joke around a lot but I took every opportunity to make sure that my actions would not disgrace God or the church I was a part of.

One day, upon arriving at the school and walking to my class, I was stopped by a student I did not know well. I believe she was visiting the school. She stopped me and she said, "Are you a Christian?" and I responded boldly "Yes, why did you ask?" and she responded, "I can see God all over you. The way you walk and talk I just knew you were a Christian and actively involved in church." I took that opportunity to talk to her about God. I cannot say that she has surrendered but I can say that her life was touched by just simply observing my actions.

In another instance, someone got baptized after I preached a sermon. After being baptized, this person shared with me that it was I who had motivated him to serve Christ. The fact that I talk about God boldly and my life reflects His will, proves to others that young men and women can serve the Lord.

I beseech you therefore, brethren, by the mercies of God: Live a life that can encourage others to serve God.

May the life you live speak for you! It will not always be easy and sometimes you will fail, mess up and slip up. But when you fall, get up, brush yourself off because someone is watching you and you may very well impact their lives positively if you live for God wholeheartedly.

Brawta Scripture

"In the same way, let your good deeds shine out for all to see so that everyone will praise your heavenly Father" (Matthew 5:16, NLT).

REFLECTION

What area of your life do you want God to help you improve?

_____

_____

_____

_____

_____

_____

Do you need to be more charitable?

_____

_____

_____

_____

_____

Do you need to be more honest?

_____

_____

_____

_____

_____

_____

Whatever the area is, I encourage you to talk to God about it.

Write to God

_____

_____

_____

_____

_____

_____

Day 7

ANSWER THE CALL TO SERVE

The text below tells us of Jeremiah's calling into ministry. It encourages us to answer God's call.

"I knew you before I formed you in your mother's womb. Before you were born, I set you apart and appointed you as my prophet to the nations" (Jeremiah 1:5, NLT).

Encouragement

Just like Jeremiah, you are called to serve. Service is not just about preaching or behind the pulpit activity. Each person in the body of Christ has a specific call on their lives to serve in ministry. Not everyone will be a preacher, a pastor or a prophet but that does not mean your calling is infinitesimal. The book of Jeremiah opens with him being called into ministry in the first chapter. Jeremiah was called into a prophetic ministry and the time of his calling was when Judah was on a journey to exile. He was called in chaos. Like many of us, our call to serve comes in a time of chaos; chaos in our lives or chaos in the lives of others.

Like Jeremiah, you may have responded to the call of God by saying you are too young or you are too old. Or you may have responded like Moses in the book of Exodus by saying you cannot speak well. Honestly, our initial response may not always be *YES, LORD*. Our human nature will have us question our capability to serve. Do not limit yourself to serve in the Kingdom of God because of your age, height, colour or statue. God looks pass all of that and just wants you to serve Him in His ministry here on earth. On Day 8, I want to talk about the job description of your call to serve. Here's a testimony below.

Testimony

I have been preaching to the pillows and beds of my house long before I got saved. I got saved in 2007 at age 14, and received the gift of tongues not many months later. I was on fire for God, but after being saved I was not asked to preach. I did every other ministry within the church I got saved in except preaching. Years later, I started my undergraduate degree in Theology and I was asked to preach at a youth convention in the hills of St. Catherine. I was excited to do that. I felt the call of God to serve and I answered the call.

I preached my first formal message on that Sabbath morning and I haven't stopped preaching since. In each season I entered, God downloaded in me an updated job description that came with my call. My latest prophetic word came to me that I was called into an Apostolic ministry. It took me months to accept this call because I felt that I was not worthy of such a calling. However, the Lord did not have the same thoughts as I had. He birthed a passion in me to want to grow churches and ministry. I was afforded the opportunity to serve my current church organization as Parish Youth Leader to give oversight to the youth ministry of 39 churches, and create plans to grow that ministry in all areas.

I beseech you therefore, brethren, by the mercies of God: Answer the call to serve.

Every ministry is different. You may be called to serve as a youth leader, praise and worship member, usher or teacher. Whatever the call on your life is, answer it. Someone is waiting for you to answer your call. Someone is looking for an usher who will greet them with a smile and make their day "light up;" a preacher who will deliver a timely and accurate word; a worship leader who will command the atmosphere to respond to the glory of God. You are being waited on so answer the call to serve today.

Brawta Scripture

"In the last days,' God says, 'I will pour out my Spirit upon all people. Your sons and daughters will prophesy. Your young men will see visions, and your old men will dream dreams" (Acts 2:17, NLT).

REFLECTION

What ministry are you called to serve in?

_____

_____

_____

_____

_____

_____

How do you know that your current ministry is where God wants you to be?

_____

_____

_____

_____

_____

_____

_____

Are you running from the call?

_____

_____

_____

_____

_____

_____

_____

_____

_____

_____

_____

_____

_____

_____

_____

_____

_____

_____

I encourage you to talk to God about your service in His ministry. Ask Him to guide you.

Write to God

_____

_____

_____

_____

_____

_____

Day 8

UNDERSTAND
WHAT YOUR TASK IS ALL ABOUT

The text below gives us a job description of Jeremiah's call and therefore encourages us to understand what our task is all about.

Then the Lord reached out and touched my mouth and said, "Look, I have put my words in your mouth! Today I appoint you to stand up against nations and kingdoms. Some you must uproot and tear down, destroy and overthrow. Others you must build up and plant" (Jeremiah 1:9-10, NLT).

Encouragement

Jeremiah got a word concerning Judah's destruction and the Lord's reconstruction of Judah. The word to Jeremiah was for him to tell Judah all that God had commanded him to say. God will never give you a ministry without giving you objectives and goals to reach. With those objectives and goals, God will give you a job description. For Jeremiah, he was told to *uproot, tear down, destroy, overthrow and build up and plant*. Jeremiah's calling was rough and we see a similar task for the prophet Isaiah in Isaiah chapter 6.

No calling is easy but it is necessary. If Jeremiah did not know what to say he would be useless to send forth into the city. God has called you to serve and I believe he has given you the necessary tools you need to serve him. You have been given a job description; write it down. The best thing in ministry is to understand what your calling is and how it can help the body of Christ and effect change in society. On Day 9, we close off the Jeremiah story by encouraging you to be dressed for the call of service.

Testimony

The Lord has called me into an apostolic ministry and has placed a great task on my hands to serve my church body. Mornings, evenings, and night the Lord would give me a vision or dream as to what my task is. For each season I would get a different task that I need to complete. The members of my committee will often get messages from me in the wee hours of the morning because some things the Lord would reveal to me, I cannot wait to share it. Today, I am like Habbakuk, I will look to see what God will say to me.

I beseech you therefore, brethren, by the mercies of God: Seek God for your task.

We all have a different call and we all have a different task. But the Kingdom of God on earth will not accomplish all if you do not know what you are called to do, and how you must effectively carry out the call.

Brawta Scripture

"I will stand at my watch and station myself on the ramparts; I will look to see what he will say to me, and what answer I am to give to this complaint" (Habakkuk 2:1, NLT).

REFLECTION

What visions and dreams have the Lord given you?

_____

_____

_____

_____

_____

_____

What has He revealed to you that you need to do to complete the task?

_____

_____

_____

_____

_____

_____

Do you know what your call to serve entails?

_____

_____

_____

_____

_____

_____

I encourage you to talk to God about your job description.

Write to God

_____

_____

_____

_____

_____

Day 9

DRESS YOURSELF FOR WORK!

The text below tells us how God prepared Jeremiah for the work he had to do. May we be encouraged to be well dressed for our work in ministry.

Get up and prepare for action. Go out and tell them everything I tell you to say. Do not be afraid of them, or I will make you look foolish in front of them. For see, today I have made you strong like a fortified city that cannot be captured, like an iron pillar or a bronze wall. You will stand against the whole land—the kings, officials, priests, and people of Judah. They will fight you, but they will fail. For I am with you, and I will take care of you.

I, the Lord, have spoken! (Jeremiah 1:17-19, NLT)

Encouragement

Our dress code for ministry is always outlined in the Bible. Whatever you are called to do you can find out how you must attire yourself. This attire is not physical, it is spiritual. You must be dressed spiritually for the task God has given you. Pray more. Fast more. Worship more. Read the word more. God has fortified you just as He did with Jeremiah and you will stand before great men and shall not be put to shame if you are properly attired. On Day 10, we change the scope of things and look at the miracle of the man at Gate Beautiful and how we must continue our work even in the streets. We will call Day 10, the after-party.

Testimony

I had a struggle to fast and it was affecting my ministry as a preacher. I was doing more than just preaching now. I was involved in deliverance ministry and I needed to be properly fortified. The Lord revealed to me that I needed to fast and pray more. I will not lie to say I have been successful on every attempt to fast and pray but I have started and I see the results. After fasting and prayer I have no problem in casting out demons and helping others break free from bondage. I believe that there is power in prayer. As a preacher, to help build my ministry, I pray more, read more and I'm learning to fast more. I have seen miracles happen when I attire myself in all the above.

I beseech you therefore, brethren, by the mercies of God: Dress well for ministry!

Pray more. Fast more. Read the word of God more. Love more. Worship more. Make sure you are always in the presence of God.

Brawta Scriptures

"Therefore, put on every piece of God's armor so you will be able to resist the enemy in the time of evil" (Ephesians 6:13, NLT).

"Pray in the Spirit at all times and on every occasion. Stay alert and be persistent in your prayers for all believers everywhere" (Ephesians 6:18, NLT).

REFLECTION

What do you need to strengthen?

_____

_____

_____

_____

_____

_____

_____

_____

What piece of the armour is missing?

_____

_____

_____

_____

_____

_____

_____

Do you need to be more dedicated to fasting just as I
need to be?

_____

_____

_____

_____

_____

_____

_____

Write to God

_____

_____

_____

_____

_____

_____

_____

_____

_____

_____

_____

Day 10

KEEP THE PARTY GOING

The text below tells us how Peter and John were going to a temple and saw a lame man. He was at the gate called Beautiful and they commanded him to walk.

"Then Peter took the lame man by the right hand and helped him up. And as he did, the man's feet and ankles were instantly healed and strengthened" (Acts of the Apostles 3:7, NLT).

Encouragement

I love the book of Acts of the Apostles. If you need any encouragement to continue the work of the Lord just read the book of Acts. Peter and John had experienced Pentecost and after such a phenomenal experience they kept the party going. Have you ever been to a party before? If you have then you may know the term "after party". The after party is usually the hype party that only includes a few people. Not everyone from the main party would be invited to the after party.

Peter and John were going by the church to worship and continue the party and on their way, they met a lame man at Gate Beautiful. Because of the Pentecost experience, they commanded the man to walk. You may have experienced a Pentecost in your life. You may have seen a miracle or experienced an open heaven. Be encouraged to take that experience with you everywhere you go. Someone is waiting on you to command them to walk. On Day 11, we stay in the book of Acts as we encourage you to use the power of the Holy Ghost.

Testimony

I remember when I went to church and the word of God, as always, was powerful. The preacher that Sunday was Rev. Valentine Rodney, a man of God I admire a great deal. He preached with such power and authority that I was captivated to hear what God had to say through him. He was sharing his sermonic thought and then he said this, "There shall be water without rain" and as he expounded, I was amazed. The very same day and the week I had to share it with others. It was too profound. I've now caused people to challenge the word and find preachers who will challenge the norm of life. I kept an after party.

I beseech you therefore, brethren, by the mercies of God: Keep the party going.

What experiences have you had with God that is worthy of sharing? You may have that experience at church or even in your prayer time. For some, it may have been at a Gospel concert. Do not be selfish, keep the party going and share that experience and testimony with others. Someone is waiting for you to keep an after party.

Brawta Scripture

"But Peter said, I don't have any silver or gold for you. But I'll give you what I have. In the name of Jesus Christ, the Nazarene, get up and walk!" (Acts of the Apostles 3:6, NLT)

REFLECTION

What experience have you had with God?

_____

_____

_____

_____

_____

_____

Have you shared it yet?

_____

_____

_____

_____

_____

_____

_____

Do you know how to share the experience with the power to change the life of others?

_____

_____

_____

_____

_____

_____

_____

Write to God

_____

_____

Day 11

USE THE POWER OF THE HOLY GHOST

The text before us shows us how Peter walked in the power of the Holy Ghost and sick bodies were healed from just his shadow.

As a result of the apostles' work, sick people were brought out into the streets on beds and mats so that Peter's shadow might fall across some of them as he went by. Crowds came from the villages around Jerusalem, bringing their sick and those possessed by evil spirits, and they were all healed (Acts of the Apostles 5:15-16, NLT)

Encouragement

The apostles were exposed to the power of God both in authority and might through the Holy Spirit. After their encounter with the Holy Ghost in Acts 2, they were empowered. Have you been exposed to the power of the Holy Ghost? If you have not yet been exposed to such awesome power, you need to get that exposure immediately and start to use the power of the Holy Ghost in everything you do. In this season, you need the power to stand firm and the only power that you can harness and give glory to God is the power of the Holy Spirit. In this season, may you operate in the power of the Holy Spirit and like Peter, may your shadow provoke healing in sick bodies. May you lay hands and cast out demons by the command of your word through the power of Almighty God.

Testimony

I have learnt that the Holy Spirit is not tongues. I've been taught that you need tongues but after proper study of scripture, I realize I needed power. The Holy Spirit is the person of God that gives us power; power to do great things. I went to service to preach and there was a demonic manifestation happening and I couldn't be still and not do anything. I prayed quietly and ask the Lord to empower me to address the demon and then I walk over to the person and commanded the demon to go. Through the power of the Holy Spirit, the Lord revealed to me the demon that was operating and I called it by name and the person was delivered.

I beseech you therefore, brethren, by the mercies of God: Use the power of the Holy Spirit.

In this season, command the things that are not as though they are. If you have the Holy Spirit you have power.

Brawta Scripture

Look, I have given you authority over all the power of the enemy, and you can walk among snakes and scorpions and crush them. Nothing will injure you. But don't rejoice because evil spirits obey you; rejoice because your names are registered in heaven (Luke 10:19-20, NLT).

REFLECTION

What do you need to speak to in your life?

_____

_____

_____

_____

_____

_____

What area of your life seems to be in disarray?

_____

_____

_____

_____

_____

_____

_____

Use the power of the Holy Ghost.

_____

_____

_____

_____

_____

_____

Write to God

_____

_____

_____

_____

Day 12

PUT YOUR FEET UP

The text below encourages us to sit at God's right hand and watch Him deal with the enemies in our lives.

"The Lord said to my Lord, 'Sit in the place of honor at my right hand until I humble your enemies, making them a footstool under your feet'" (Psalms 110:1, NLT).

Encouragement

We have been through rough days in our lives and it's common to have hiccups every now and then in the race of life. Throughout life, there may have been some ups and downs, also there may have been some defeats but I am positive that there have been victories. This is encouraging for you. Yes, you may have been through the chaos of life. You may be tired from fighting battles that you did not choose to fight. In this season God is telling us through His word to just relax. Sit back and put your feet up. Watch the hand of God work in your life and whatever the problems are hand them over to God today. Make today the day you relax in the hand of God, put your feet up and watch God humble your enemies, making them your footstool. On Day 12, we will explore the story of the "Potter and the Clay" and show you how God wants to mould you into His perfect masterpiece.

Testimony

This is short but I hope you are encouraged. I see where God has made the enemy my footstool. I have been given time to backslide and time to die. My life had its chaos and I believe the enemy was happy but the same folks who were speaking negatively over my life are now seeking my help so they can become something good in society. Be encouraged in this season, God is making the enemy your footstool.

I beseech you therefore, brethren, by the mercies of God: Put your feet up.

In this season relax in the joy of the Lord and watch God deal with the enemies in your life.

Brawta Scripture

O Lord, I have so many enemies; so many are against me. So many are saying, "God will never rescue him!" But you, O Lord, are a shield around me; you are my glory, the one who holds my head high *(Psalms 3:1-3, NLT)*.

REFLECTION

What are some troubles that you have encountered in the past and you wish not to encounter them today?

_____

_____

_____

_____

_____

_____

Let's talk to God about it.

_____

_____

_____

_____

_____

_____

_____

_____

_____

_____

Write to God

_____

_____

_____

_____

_____

_____

_____

_____

_____

Day 13

BE LIKE CLAY IN GOD'S HANDS

The text below tells us about the story of a potter and the clay. In this season may you be like clay in the hand of God: easily moulded for His purpose.

The Lord gave another message to Jeremiah. He said, "Go down to the potter's shop, and I will speak to you there." So, I did as he told me and found the potter working at his wheel. But the jar he was making did not turn out as he had hoped, so he crushed it into a lump of clay again and started over (Jeremiah 18:1-4, NLT).

Encouragement

It has often been said that as human beings we are imperfect and prone to faults. We cannot necessarily contest such a statement because if you are true to yourself you would agree that this is true. In our human nature, there is no perfection. Because of the fall of man in the book of Genesis we have been doomed to experience a life of mistakes, regrets, struggles, troubles, hurts and pain. We make mistakes as human beings and sometimes the consequences are tough but we face them nonetheless. You may have been broken, battered and bruised in the past season but in this season may you be like the clay in the text. The clay in the text was marred in the Potter's hand just as you and I are marred sometimes.

The clay can represent us in our state of depression and dismay. It represents us in our state of brokenness. It represents us in our state of pain. The clay was marred but the Potter did not dispose of it. Sometimes in our lives, we are going to be marred and messed up but rest assured that God will never dispose of us. The clay did not give any trouble in the hand of the potter. The clay had purpose like you and me. You may think that you are messed up and have no use again but that is a lie from the pit of hell. The potter wants to mould you into the perfect being. In the same way, the clay represents us, so too the Potter represents God. In this season may God re-mould you. Your last season may have left you broken, bruised and marred but be clay in God's hand and watch God mould you into the best version of you.

Testimony

I made some mistakes in my life, like all of us, and although I was preaching, I felt like I was not worthy to preach again. Life had begun to overwhelm me but I decided I was going to go to God and ask God to make me over. Today, I write to you as clay that has been re-moulded. And whenever I get bruised, I remind myself that the Potter still has the power to re-mould me. In this season, be clay in the hands of the Master Potter -God Almighty.

I beseech you therefore, brethren, by the mercies of God: Be like a lump of clay in the God's hand.

Just as the potter chose to not throw away the clay, so too God will not throw you away. Be like clay and let God re-mould you.

Brawta Scripture

"And yet, O Lord, you are our Father. We are the clay, and you are the potter. We all are formed by your hand" (Isaiah 64:8, NLT).

REFLECTION

Where have you been bruised?

_____

_____

_____

_____

_____

_____

_____

_____

Who was it that bruised you?

_____

_____

_____

_____

_____

_____

How do you see yourself today?

_____

_____

_____

_____

_____

_____

_____

Let's talk to God about it.

Write to God

_____

_____

_____

_____

_____

_____

_____

_____

Day 14

LAUNCH OUT INTO THE DEEP

The text below tells us about some fishermen being sent out into the deep to get a better catch. May we launch out into the deep in this season for the big catch.

"When he had finished speaking, he said to Simon, "Now go out where it is deeper, and let down your nets to catch some fish" (Luke 5:4, NLT)

Encouragement

Luke 5 speaks volumes on obeying the word of God. The fishermen were toiling all night and caught no fish at all. Jesus then gave them a great command to go deeper. Jesus was teaching on the seashore and he saw two ships that had already docked and the fishermen were washing their nets. The fishermen washing their nets was a sign that they were finished working. It could also be a sign that they had given up. Jesus turned to one of the fishermen known as Simon and encouraged him to launch out further from land. He encouraged him to go into the deep.

Are you about to wash your net? If you are, I am encouraging you, as Jesus did with Simon, to go into the deep. Never give up. Have faith that something will happen and launch out at the command of God. The deep holds greater miracles. The deep may very well have the breakthrough that you have been praying about. It's time to launch out.

Testimony

I worked as a Guidance Counsellor for almost two years with the Ministry of Education, Youth and Information in two different institutions. They were not permanent posts and my tenure had come to an end. I became a relief announcer with LOVE 101 FM Jamaica's number 1 Gospel station and in that season, I was asked to be on staff as a producer and a main announcer. I was elated and accepted the offer but in the year 2018, I had to launch out. I prayed and made a decision to resign from being a producer. It was tough but I did it. I launched out not knowing what would happen. Before 2019 came into full effect, I received an email to be a Master Trainer with the Ministry of Education, Youth and Information to assist in training five thousand people to work in the BPO Industry. My advice to you is this: when God gives you the command to launch out, do it.

I beseech you therefore, brethren, by the mercies of God: Take the risk and launch out into the deep by faith.

In launching out you need to trust God and be bold. Nothing comes to those who sit on the shallow part of life but everything will come to those who obey God. If he commands you to, launch out. Do it. In this season may you be obedient and launch out upon the command of God and may you see the hand of God move mightily in your life.

Brawta Scripture

Farmers who wait for perfect weather never plant. If they watch every cloud, they never harvest. Just as you cannot understand the path of the wind or the mystery of a tiny baby growing in its mother's womb, so you cannot understand the activity of God, who does all things. Plant your seed in the morning and keep busy all afternoon, for you don't know if profit will come from one activity or another—or maybe both (Ecclesiastes 11:4-6, NLT).

REFLECTION

What haven't you accomplished in your last season?

_____

_____

_____

_____

_____

_____

_____

Are you washing your net?

_____

_____

_____

_____

_____

_____

Have you given up?

_____

_____

_____

_____

_____

_____

_____

_____

I implore you to launch out today. Let's talk to God.

Write to God

_____

_____

_____

_____

_____

_____

_____

_____

_____

Day 15

TAKE RISKS WITH CHRIST

The text below shows Peter's courage when he stepped out of the boat to walk to Jesus on the water.

"Yes, come," Jesus said. So, Peter went over the side of the boat and walked on the water toward Jesus" (Matthew 14:29, NLT).

Encouragement

We will take three days to cover this story. Today, let's talk about taking risks with Christ.

Peter is on the boat with some friends and Jesus saw them struggling with the winds. They were on a journey where the water was between two mountains or hills (vs.23) so the breeze was heavy. Jesus walked on the water to them and said to Peter, "Come." Peter was brave enough to inquire whether the image before them was Jesus or a ghost. Jesus confirmed and Peter took the risk and walked out of the boat and stepped on top of the water.

In this season, may we take risks like Peter. We launched out on Day 14. Now, we are encouraged to take bold risks On Day 15. Jesus is calling us out of complacency and He is saying come and experience greater things in this season. Are you comfortable in the boat you are in? If you are, take the risk and step out. God wants to show you great things and you'll only see it if you take the risk. No risk, no faith. On Day 16 we continue this interesting story to encourage you not to take your eyes off Jesus.

Testimony

In college, I started my studies in Guidance and Counselling. I told myself "I was sure to have a job with that degree and it would be a well-paying job as well." In my second year of study though, the Lord, through a lecturer and also through prayer told me to change my degree. I was encouraged to study Theology. Others told me that studying Theology wouldn't give me a good job. I minored in Guidance and Counselling and took the risk and did my major in Theology. I decided to take the risk with Christ. I graduated in 2016, and worked in two institutions as a Guidance Counsellor as previously mentioned. Currently, I am working in the radio field as a radio personality. I am preaching and teaching others the Bible. I took the risk and God honored my move. I encourage you to take the risk with Christ.

I beseech you therefore, brethren, by the mercies of God: take risks with God.

At some point on your Christian journey, you are going to be placed in a position that will challenge your faith. This faith challenging position requires that risks be taken. Once you know that God is directing you and holding on to your hands, take the risk.

Brawta Scripture

"For I know the plans I have for you," says the Lord. "They are plans for good and not for disaster, to give you a future and a hope" (Jeremiah 29:11, NLT).

REFLECTION

What are some risks you are willing to take with God?

_____

_____

_____

_____

_____

_____

What boat of complacency do you need to step out of?

_____

_____

_____

_____

_____

_____

_____

Remember, God has a plan for you and all you need to do is trust God and take the risk and step out of the boat. Let's talk to God.

Write to God

_____

_____

_____

_____

_____

_____

_____

_____

_____

_____

Day 16

STAY FOCUSED

Continuing the story of Peter walking on the water; this aspect of the text encourages us to not take our eyes off Jesus.

"But when he saw the strong wind and the waves, he was terrified and began to sink. 'Save me, Lord!' he shouted" (Matthew 14:30, NLT).

Encouragement

You must try your best to keep your focus on Jesus. Peter stepped out of the boat in faith and walked towards Jesus. While walking towards Jesus he saw the strong wind and waves. We all have been in precarious positions as that of Peter. We are walking to Jesus but the winds and waves of life sometimes look and sound terrifying. It's normal to be fearful but in the midst of the fear never take your eyes off Jesus.

Peter was terrified and he began to sink. Sometimes we sink in our own fear. Remember, "God has not given you the spirit of fear, but power, love and a sound mind" (1Timothy 1:7). Truly we have all been there where we started sinking in our waves of fears and winds of depression. If ever we take our eyes off Jesus, we will sink. That's just a fact. In this season, you will encounter new waves and new winds but try your very best to not take your eyes off Jesus, but if you do look away because of fear, Day 18 will help us to understand that God will quickly save us.

Testimony

The story of Peter stands as the best testimony to use. When he took his eyes off Jesus, he began to sink but when he cried out to Christ he received help. In this season, may you not sink in fear but stay focused on Jesus. In my ministry of preaching and teaching, I fell down on reading the scriptures and praying. I started to sink in complacency. I was not very focused on God until I developed the courage to cry out. In my crying out, God helped me to create a strategic way of praying and reading and at this very moment, my eyes are focused on Jehovah.

I beseech you therefore, brethren, by the mercies of God: Stay focused.

The winds and waves will come but remain focused on God in this season and you will never sink.

Brawta Scripture

"Look straight ahead, and fix your eyes on what lies before you" (Proverbs 4:25, NLT).

REFLECTION

What are the wind and waves that are grabbing for your attention?

_____

_____

_____

_____

_____

_____

What is distracting you on your walk with God?

_____

_____

_____

_____

_____

_____

Let's talk to God about it.

Write to God

_____

_____

_____

_____

_____

_____

_____

_____

_____

_____

Day 17

CRY OUT TO GOD

In our final look at the story of Peter walking to Jesus, we are encouraged in the text below to cry out to God when we have lost focus.

But when he saw the strong wind and the waves, he was terrified and began to sink. "Save me, Lord!" he shouted. Jesus immediately reached out and grabbed him. "You have so little faith," Jesus said. "Why did you doubt me?" (Matthew 14:30-31, NLT).

Encouragement

Peter got distracted as we stated on Day 17. He started to sink because of the fear due to him hearing and seeing the wind and the waves. While Peter was sinking, he shouted to Jesus for rescue. Like many of us, we sink at times but be encouraged to shout to God for help. Forget the fears and cry out as loudly as possible. God hears every prayer you pray. He sees your need. He feels your pain. Jesus reached out to Peter and pulled him up and addressed his faith. Peter is like you and me. Sometimes doubt arises and it pushes us down. In this season, may your faith be strong and may you cry out to God in every single case of fear. Jesus heard you and He wants to pull you out of your sinking position.

Testimony

I was diagnosed with minor epileptic shocks. After doing all the tests I was told that there was no evidence of epilepsy. I was having the shocks and fear took over. I did not want to be alone. I was scared of the dark and if I saw a shadow, I thought I was going to be shocked. After going through prayer, I decided that I could not live in a sunken state. I boldly cried out to Jesus and declared I am healed. Today, I write to you as a healed man, not taking any medication and I haven't had even a hint of epileptic shock in years. I encourage you to cry out to God.

I beseech you therefore, brethren, by the mercies of God: Cry out for help.

Jesus wants us to cry out to Him. He will not shun us. He will help us and correct us. In this season I pray that you'll call out to Jesus for help when you need it.

Brawta Scripture

"I took my troubles to the Lord; I cried out to Him, and He answered my prayer" (Psalms 120:1, NLT).

REFLECTION

What sunken state are you in at the moment?

_____

_____

_____

_____

_____

_____

What's pulling you down?

_____

_____

_____

_____

_____

_____

_____

I dare you to cry out for help. Let's talk to God.

_____

_____

_____

_____

_____

_____

Write to God

_____

_____

_____

_____

Day 18

RUN

The scripture below encourages us to make a run for it when we find ourselves in a compromising situation.

One day, however, no one else was around when he went in to do his work. She came and grabbed him by his cloak, demanding, "Come on, sleep with me!" Joseph tore himself away, but he left his cloak in her hand as he ran from the house (Genesis 39: 11-12, NLT).

Encouragement

In the Jamaican culture, the word "run" has more than one connotations to it. You run to win or you run to save your life. In the text before us, the run was one to save

Joseph's life. Potiphar's wife had a great interest in Joseph because he was younger, presumably thick and very handsome. She wanted to get closer to Joseph, dishonor her husband and also would have caused Joseph to dishonor his boss. Like Joseph, some of us find ourselves in precarious situations in life. We encounter a sticky situation that can jeopardize a friendship, relationship, family or even marriage.

Joseph saw the plot of Potiphar's wife and he ran in order to save himself. It is best to have persons talk about you with false evidence than to have them talk about you because you have yielded to the temptation. Potiphar's wife grabbed the cloak of Joseph and told a great lie on him, but Joseph knew he was innocent and he knew God was going to deliver him from the lies that were told on him. If you find yourself in a situation that will have you to lean into temptation, RUN. Run because it is the best thing for you to do to maintain your integrity.

Testimony

Just like Joseph, I found myself in a precarious situation. It was while I was in college. She was beautiful and spoke intelligently. Beauty and conversational skills are what I admire in a woman. I served my college in my final year as Student Council President and so I had an office space. The first office space was located by the Student Union and this very student came to my office to ask me to advocate for her grade. Naïve as I was, I entertained the conversation and welcomed her into the office.

We sat and I heard her concern and gave her the direction she needed to follow up with querying the grade that she had a problem with. She broke down before me and I felt it necessary to extend a hug to her as a mean of comforting her because she said she was overwhelmed by the low grade she received. In that same moment, she lifted her head and kissed me. Remember, she has beauty and brain, the things that get me weak. The thoughts that ran through my mind were not as holy I expected them to be. I quickly came to my senses, eased her off and she apologized while moving closer to me. The secluded area to where my first office was located was a good spot for anything to happen with no one being caught. I was not about to smear my name and the office of president for the Student Council.

I escorted her out of the office and out of the student lounge and went back inside to breathe. Days later, I was considered a "wuss" in other words she told her friends that I was a coward and could not handle her. My running away from that situation was a good move for me because she was struggling with trust issues and if anything had happened, I know she would have been hurt to the core and most of all I would have sinned against God. Running sometimes is the best option. I encourage you to run whenever you find yourself in tempting situations.

I beseech you therefore, brethren, by the mercies of God: Run from temptation!

You will be ridiculed when you do so. You will be laughed at and mocked. They may even tell lies on you but once you know you have not sinned against God, He (God) will avenge you. Run if you have to.

Brawta Scripture

"So, I say, let the Holy Spirit guide your lives. Then you won't be doing what your sinful nature craves" (Galatians 5:16, NLT).

REFLECTION

What tempting situation have you found yourself falling into over and over?

_____

_____

_____

_____

_____

What do you believe is your biggest temptation?

_____

_____

_____

_____

_____

_____

_____

How have you dealt with fleeing/running from that temptation?

_____

_____

_____

_____

_____

Let's talk to God.

Write to God

Tell God the temptations that come daily and ask Him to help you flee from them

_____

_____

_____

Day 19

REJOICE IN HARDSHIP (PART 1)

Note: We will take three days to talk about rejoicing in tribulations.

The text below encourages us to be glad when we encounter tribulation.

"We can rejoice, too, when we run into problems and trials, for we know that they help us develop endurance" (Romans 5:3, NLT).

Encouragement

When one hears or sees the word "rejoice," what often comes to mind is victory. This is because it is normal for one to rejoice after obtaining victory. It is normal for us as human beings to be glad when things are going in our favour. However, we are encouraged to rejoice not during victorious times, but in trials and problems. We all have those days when we encounter some level of tribulation. But in the tribulation we encounter we are encouraged to boast. It seems impossible at times to rejoice in hardship and suffering but the apostle Paul is saying that it is the best time to rejoice. Rejoice in tribulation because it produces endurance.

Endurance is synonymous with the word perseverance. And perseverance means to actually do something despite the difficulty. The reason we must rejoice in tribulation is that it builds our level of endurance. What you are going through is not designed to kill you but it is designed to build you and to develop perseverance in you. Rejoice in the tribulation because God is there with you and God will not leave you to die in hardship. In this season of hardship, I pray that you will develop endurance. On Day 20, we will look at developing character in hardship.

Testimony

I experienced a rough patch in my life when I had no permanent job. I have never been out of work for more than three months after leaving college but I never had a full-time position. I wanted a car so badly but could not get one because I had no permanent post to take out a loan. This season was rough for me because I was asked to speak almost every week at different churches across the island and renting a vehicle was not financially viable.

In that season, I felt down but then I remembered that all things work together for good (Romans 8:28) and I began to rejoice. I rented cars and rejoiced knowing that one day I would have my own. I developed endurance in that season. Today, I am driving my own vehicle and thanking God that during the hardship of taking the bus to preaching engagements and renting vehicles to go far distances, He provided for me. I pray that you will rejoice in the hardship because it will produce endurance in you.

I beseech you therefore, brethren, by the mercies of God: Rejoice in hardship because it will build endurance in you.

When life seems hard and difficult to manage, rejoice. Around the corner, God has an answer for you. He is just helping you to build up your level of endurance.

Brawta Scripture

"Always be full of joy in the Lord. I say it again-rejoice!" (Philippians 4:4, NLT)

REFLECTION

What are some hardships that you are facing?

_____

_____

_____

_____

_____

_____

What is it that seems difficult in your life?

_____

_____

_____

_____

_____

_____

_____

Let's talk to God about it.

Write to God

_____

_____

_____

_____

_____

_____

_____

_____

_____

_____

Day 20

REJOICE IN HARDSHIP (PART 2)

Not only does rejoicing in tribulation develop endurance but the continued text below encourages us that it also builds character.

"And endurance develops strength of character…" (Romans 5:4A, NLT).

Encouragement

The word "character" in the text can be used synonymously with the word experience. Paul tells us that we must rejoice in hardship because after going through the hardship we will develop and have enough experience to testify that God can take a person through anything. Rejoice because your tribulation builds your testimony and your testimony affects your character and your character is proof that what you have been through did not break you but helped to develop you. After going through hardship people will see you and know that you are a survivor. In this season, your character will be built. While you are experiencing the pressure of the hard times, rejoice because it is building you into being the person God wants you to be. On Day 21, we will look at how your hope is built during hardship.

Testimony

I served as a Guidance Counsellor in a school located in a volatile area. This was a test to build character. I had to encounter students from different communities with different intentions. My Christian character was being tested. I was being pushed by the behaviour of the students to act out of character and hit them or curse them. In this season, I learnt that my character was being built. I held my head up and stood my ground and I survived. Later, went to another institution with far greater tests than the first one, but at this institution, my character was built and nothing shifted my focus. To this day, I am respected in both schools. Through the hardship with teachers and students, my character was built. In this season, I pray that your character will be built from every experience you have.

I beseech you therefore, brethren, by the mercies of God: Rejoice in hardship because it helps us to develop endurance and endurance develops character.

Your experience can make or break you. In this season of your life, I pray you will not be broken down by hardship but you will develop great strength of character.

Brawta Scripture

"So, let it grow, for when your endurance is fully developed, you will be perfect and complete, needing nothing" (James 1:4, NLT).

REFLECTION

What are you enduring that you believe is building your character?

_____

_____

_____

_____

_____

_____

Do you see yourself developing well?

_____

_____

_____

_____

_____

_____

_____

Let's talk to God.

Write to God

_____

_____

_____

_____

_____

_____

_____

_____

_____

_____

Day 21

DEVELOP YOUR HOPE IN HARDSHIP

The final part of our tribulation series talks about building our hope. The text below says that character strengthens our hope of salvation.

"And character strengthens our confident hope of salvation. And this hope will not lead to disappointment" (Romans 5:4b-5a, NLT).

Encouragement

The word hope in this text can mean confidence in God. Paul is, therefore, encouraging us to rejoice in hardship because it gives us confidence in God. Hope and faith go hand in hand. The book of Hebrews tells us that faith is the thing that we are confident in God for. So, rejoice in tribulation because it develops endurance, and endurance develops character and character develops confidence and hope in God. Your hope must be built on Jesus and nothing else. Everything else will fail but if we build our hope on Jesus, the text tells us that we will never be put to shame or disappointment. Therefore, when things are good, rejoice. When things are bad, rejoice. When you feel like hardship is unending, rejoice because it is here to build you and build your hope in God.

Testimony

On Day 21, you are encouraged to write your testimony. What has developed your endurance, character and hope in God? How do you handle hardship? What is the scripture that keeps you going?
Testify below:

_____

_____

_____

_____

_____

_____

_____

_____

_____

_____

_____

_____

I beseech you therefore, brethren, by the mercies of God: Develop confidence in God.

You can only develop confidence when you endure hardship. Do not despise the hard times but rejoice in them.

REFLECTION

What hardship are you currently being faced with?

_____

_____

_____

_____

_____

_____

_____

How do you plan to overcome hardship?

_____

_____

_____

_____

_____

_____

_____

On Day 21 you are encouraged to talk to God in prayer by telling him thanks for the hardship of life that has and is still developing you.

Write to God

Dear Lord Jesus...

_____

_____

_____

_____

_____

_____

_____

_____

_____

Day 22

DO NOT WATCH THE OPPOSITION

Note: In this three-part encouragement we will look at Nehemiah and the rebuilding of the wall.

The text below shows us that we will have oppositions when doing good things.

Sanballat was very angry when he learned that we were rebuilding the wall. He flew into a rage and mocked the Jews, saying in front of his friends and the Samarian army officers, "What does this bunch of poor, feeble Jews think they're doing? Do they think they can build the wall in a single day by just offering a few sacrifices? Do they actually think they can make something of stones from a rubbish heap—and charred ones at that?" Tobiah the Ammonite, who was standing beside him, remarked, "That stone wall would collapse if even a fox walked along the top of it! (Nehemiah 4:1-3, NLT)

Encouragement

Nehemiah started rebuilding the wall that was destroyed and that was a great and noble move of his. In the process of doing that Nehemiah had some opponents by the names Sanballat and Tobiah who mocked the process and even the progress of the rebuilding of the city's wall. However, Nehemiah did not let the opposition get the upper hand. He did not retreat from the work he set out to do. You may have started a good work like Nehemiah and probably you are currently facing opposition. Take this encouragement, do not watch them. In this season, may the opposition you may be experiencing encourage you to complete the task you have started. If you listen to every negative thought, you will fail therefore block your ears from negativity and follow through with your plan. On Day 23, I will share with you a strategy to win in rebuilding your wall.

Testimony

After being baptized at my first church which I will leave nameless, I expressed to them my passion for ministry and I was told on more than one occasion that I was not ready for the preaching ministry. I started my degree in Theology years later, and went back to the youth leader. Again I was discouraged from doing preaching ministry. They had been selecting persons who had no passion for doing it but they said I was not ready. I ended up starting a little Bible class and it was said that I wanted to start my own church. Again, the discouraging words came but I ignored them. Today, I have transferred membership after years of serving my previous church, and now I am assisting in church growth. Do not let opposition discourage you from doing the work God has called you to do. In this season, do not watch oppositions.

I beseech you therefore, brethren, by the mercies of God: Do not watch the faces of others.

Shun negativity and rebuke discouraging words. In this season, listen to the voice of God and not to the opposition.

Brawta Scripture

"They all made plans to come and fight against Jerusalem and throw us into confusion. But we prayed to our God and guarded the city day and night to protect ourselves" (Nehemiah 4:8-9, NLT).

REFLECTION

What is the opposition saying to and about you?

_____

_____

_____

_____

_____

_____

What discouraging words are they throwing at you?

_____

_____

_____

_____

_____

_____

_____

Pray to God like Nehemiah and ask God to guard you and your ministry. Let's talk to God.

Write to God

_____

_____

_____

_____

_____

_____

_____

_____

_____

Day 23

BE STRATEGIC

The text below shows us how Nehemiah developed a strategy to finish building the wall. We are encouraged to be strategic!

When our enemies heard that we knew of their plans and that God had frustrated them, we all returned to our work on the wall. But from then on, only half my men worked while the other half stood guard with spears, shields, bows, and coats of mail. The leaders stationed themselves behind the people of Judah who were building the wall. The laborers carried on their work with one hand supporting their load and one hand holding a weapon. All the builders had a sword belted to their side. The trumpeter stayed with me to sound the alarm (Nehemiah 4:15-18, NLT).

Encouragement

Nehemiah realized that the enemy had devised a plan to come and kill them all but he prayed to God for His protection. I encourage you to always pray to God for His protection. The enemy is always coming at the believers but prayer works. Nehemiah prayed and then he developed a strategy. God is strategic. If you look at the working of Almighty you will realize that God always has a plan and a strategy. Being made in God's image and likeness we too must be strategic. Nehemiah came up with a plan. Some will sleep and some will work. This plan was perfect and on Day 24, we will speak about the completion of the wall. Be encouraged in this season to be strategic. Go to the drawing board and design a strategy for your life. Make it plain upon tablets (write it down). How you will complete your goals and accomplish your vision without fear of the enemy coming in to destroy you? In this season, strategy is the key.

Testimony

In writing this book my biggest enemy was procrastination. I did not even realize that I would reach Day 23 in the course of two days! I supervise a youth ministry, work in the corporate world and am currently doing my masters. I had to develop a strategy to complete this task so that you could have this book in your hand or on your device to read and be encouraged. I prayed and asked the Lord for a strategy. I work in the afternoon hours, so the Lord revealed to me a strategic way to complete the book.

These strategic ways came out of a discussion with other authors and also through prayer and hard thinking. I would get up in the morning and write at least four encouragements. The night before bed, I would write another four. A brilliant idea came to mind to sync my devices together so that during the day when I had free time I would write as well. I ended up completing more encouragements than I had planned and rebuked procrastination. I encourage you to develop a strategic plan and stick to it.

I beseech you therefore, brethren, by the mercies of God: Be strategic in this season of your life.

Do not be easily figured out in this season. Be strategic and let people wonder. Not everyone should know your plans because not everyone wants your plans to come to pass.

Brawta Scripture

"Commit your work to the Lord, and your plans will be established" (Proverbs 16:3, ESV).

REFLECTION

What are you trying to accomplish?

_____

_____

_____

_____

_____

_____

_____

_____

Do you have a strategy?

_____

_____

_____

_____

_____

_____

_____

How will you complete it?

_____

_____

_____

_____

_____

_____

_____

_____

Let's talk to God and ask for His help.

Write to God

Seek Him for a strategy:
(In this writing, ask the Lord to reveal to you a strategy in a dream, a vision, a prophetic word or illumination of His written word)

_____

_____

_____

_____

_____

_____

_____

_____

Day 24

COMPLETE WHAT YOU HAVE STARTED

The verse below tells us how Nehemiah completed the wall. Be encouraged to complete what you have started.

So on October 2nd the wall was finished— just fifty-two days after we had begun. When our enemies and the surrounding nations heard about it, they were frightened and humiliated. They realized this work had been done with the help of our God (Nehemiah 6:15-16, NLT).

Encouragement

The wall is finished. After all Nehemiah had been through, he did not give up on the vision of finishing the wall. He worked for fifty-two days strategically avoiding the opposition. The opposition slandered him and the team but they completed the task. What have you been working on? I encourage you to be like Nehemiah and do not stop until you are finished. The enemies heard and they were put to shame. In this season, God is going to put your enemies to shame because you have been dedicated to the work. Never give up, and never stop until you have completed that which you have started.

Testimony

In spinning off the testimony, I shared about my strategic plan in writing this book. I can safely say that you are reading this book because I decided I would not stop until I completed it. I always thought that I was not called to write but God has birthed something in me and more books are to come. I have decided that this will be the first of many and there you go, you are reading a completed work. Let this serve as an encouragement, complete what you have started.

I beseech you therefore, brethren, by the mercies of God: Complete the work you have started.

There will be times when you feel overwhelmed but with the help of God, you will complete and you will be proud of yourself. Victory is yours, complete the work.

Brawta Scripture

"And I am certain that God, who began the good work within you, will continue his work until it is finally finished on the day when Christ Jesus returns" (Philippians 1:6, NLT).

REFLECTION

Are you almost finished with the task?

_____

_____

_____

_____

_____

_____

Have you placed it on hold?

_____

_____

_____

_____

_____

_____

Did you pause any at all?

_____

_____

_____

_____

_____

_____

I encourage you to continue the work until you are finished. Let's talk to God and ask Him for strength to complete the task.

Write to God

_____

_____

Day 25

BE STRONG AND VERY COURAGEOUS

The text below shows us of a conversation between God and Joshua. God encourages Joshua just as God did with Moses. You are encouraged to be strong and very courageous.

"Above all, be strong and very courageous. Be careful to observe all the law My servant Moses commanded you. Do not turn from it to the right or to the left, so that you may prosper wherever you go" (Joshua 1:7, BSB).

Encouragement

The book of Joshua is very interesting. It starts out by telling us about the death of Moses, and how Joshua is called into becoming the successor to lead the people of God into the Promised Land. In the book of Joshua, we read about the conquest of the land, the defeat of the Canaanites and the destruction of the Jericho wall. Joshua had a hard task because he had to deal with the children of Israel who were rebellious, stiff-necked and loved to complain. Not only did he have to deal with the children of Israel but he had enemies to deal with as well. God knew all of this and throughout chapter 1 of Joshua, God encouraged Joshua more than once to **be strong and very courageous.**

Just like Joshua, you may have been given a difficult task at work, school or church. You may have to lead people who are not the easiest to deal with. You may have oppositions just as Joshua had giants, but in all of that, I bring to you the encouraging word God gave to both Moses and Joshua, **be strong and very courageous.** You can only be strong in the Lord in order to succeed. Do not depart from the word of God because it is in the word of God that you will find the necessary tools to build your strength and your courage. In this season of conquest, be strong and very courageous. Do not be daunted by the faces of others; Jehovah is with you.

Testimony

I had an issue with a minister once when selecting a team of people to work with. The minister is a wonderful person but his views on a teammate were obscured and I would not accept it. I would have to talk to senior members of a ministerial team to get the consent I needed. Once I see potential in someone, I work hard to make sure that the person develops what God has placed in them. At that moment, I had to be strong and courageous because I was attempting to challenge a minister of the Lord about their views on someone. I rose to the challenge and to date the person is doing well in ministry. If God has revealed something to you that you need to defend, be strong and very courageous in doing so.

I beseech you therefore, brethren, by the mercies of God: Do not be afraid but be strong and very courageous.

Fear cripples but strength and courage push us to be bold and true. In this season, be strong and courageous and conquer the battle ahead.

Brawta Scripture

"A final word; Be strong in the Lord and in His mighty power" (Ephesians 6:10, NLT).

REFLECTION

What conquest are you on?

_____

_____

_____

_____

_____

_____

_____

What defence do you need to make?

_____

_____

_____

_____

_____

_____

Whom are you leading?

_____

_____

_____

_____

_____

_____

_____

To develop your strength and courage, let us pray to the Lord.

_____

_____

_____

_____

_____

_____

_____

Write to God

_____

_____

_____

_____

_____

_____

Day 26

DO NOT SIT WHERE YOU ARE AND DIE: MOVE

The text below shows us the faith of some lepers who risked their lives to survive. In this season do not sit in your low state and wait to die, get up and move out.

Now there were four men with leprosy sitting at the entrance of the city gates. "Why should we sit here waiting to die?" they asked each other. "We will starve if we stay here, but with the famine in the city, we will starve if we go back there. So we might as well go out and surrender to the Aramean army. If they let us live, so much the better. But if they kill us, we would have died anyway." So at twilight, they set out for the camp of the Arameans. But when they came to the edge of the camp, no one was there! For the Lord had caused the Aramean army to hear the clatter of speeding chariots and the galloping of horses and the sounds of a great army approaching. "The king of Israel has hired the Hittites and Egyptians to attack us!" they cried to one another. So they panicked and ran into the night, abandoning their tents, horses, donkeys, and everything else, as they fled for their lives. When the lepers arrived at the edge of the camp, they went into one tent after another, eating and drinking wine; and they carried off silver and gold and clothing and hid it. Finally, they said to each other, "This is not right. This is a day of good news, and we aren't sharing it with anyone! If we wait until morning, some calamity will certainly fall upon us. Come on, let's go back and tell the people at the palace (2 Kings 7:3-8).

Encouragement

The Bible said that these men were at the entrance of the gate to the city. They were lepers and therefore they were now outcasts. The law in the Old Testament given in Leviticus 13:46 said they should remain on the outskirts of the city until they die. They were left stranded on the outside of the city, sick and about to face famine. Their only option seemed to be to get up and move out. In reality, they had three options. Like some of us, we have multiple options in our decision-making and it is for us to choose the best one.

Option one for the lepers was to go back into the city. This screamed instant death because they were now outcasts, and the city was being struck by famine. Option two was to stay at the gate and just die. Options one and two for the men were never good options so they had to put forward a third option. The third option was to go into the camp of the Syrians and try to find food there in order to survive. This option was scary because the Syrians were the enemy but they refused to sit and die.

On Day 27, we will look at what happened to them in the camp of the Syrians. In this season, lay out your options for survival and through prayer and fasting choose the best one but never sit and accept defeat.

Testimony

I had the opportunity to interview many persons on my radio programme, and throughout this book I will share some of their testimonies. One of my guests shared with me that she had a problem with her hand and her doctor gave her a particular diagnosis. Medical expenses for surgery would amount to over One Hundred Thousand Jamaican dollars. She was in a position to do the surgery or trust God. She went to a concert and lifted her hands in worship and at that moment she experienced the power of God. She decided she would not sit and accept the report of the doctor to do a surgery that would cost her more than what she could afford, so she made up in her mind to trust God. Today, she is healed and touching lives across the globe through her work and ministry. Her name is Marjaalaine Francis, host of Moment of Hope aired on LOVE 101 FM Sundays at 7:30 am.

I beseech you therefore, brethren, by the mercies of God: Do not sit and die where you are: MOVE.

Put forth your options for survival and make the best choice with God at the forefront.

Brawta Scripture

"We can make our plans, but the LORD determines our steps" (Proverbs 16:9, NLT).

REFLECTION

What is the situation you are now in?

_____

_____

_____

_____

_____

_____

What are the options you have before you?

_____

_____

_____

_____

_____

Which of them seem to be the best ones?

Have you prayed about it?

_____

_____

Answer these questions in your talk with God.

Write to God

Tell Him your plans and seek His direction:

Option 1

_____

_____

_____

_____

_____

_____

Option 2

_____

_____

_____

_____

_____

_____

Option 3

_____

_____

_____

_____

_____

Pray and write down the response of God.

God's answer:

_____

_____

_____

Day 27

THE MOVE YOU MAKE MIGHT BE YOUR BEST MOVE

Continuing the story of the lepers in the book of Kings, they are now in the Syrian's camp. The text below proves that God will back our bold moves once He gives consent.

So, at twilight, they set out for the camp of the Arameans. But when they came to the edge of the camp, no one was there! For the Lord had caused the Aramean army to hear the clatter of speeding chariots and the galloping of horses and the sounds of a great army approaching. "The king of Israel has hired the Hittites and Egyptians to attack us!" they cried to one another. So they panicked and ran into the night, abandoning their tents, horses, donkeys, and everything else, as they fled for their lives (2 Kings 7:5-7, NLT).

Encouragement

The Lord sanctioned the move of the lepers. They were now in the camp of the Syrians, and no soldier was there to hinder their survival because the Lord had chased them away. Once God sanctions your bold move, He will keep you safe. The decision to move into the Syrians camp was brave and even looked stupid, but God decided that He would not let the lepers die in their situation. They weighed their options of survival and made a decision and it paid off. The camp was abandoned and the lepers had the joy of eating food and selecting beautiful, expensive clothes to wear. Providence ordered it. It was by Divine providence which is the governance of God by which God, with wisdom and love, cares for and directs all things in the universe. The doctrine of providence asserts that God is in total control of all things. Therefore, it is without a doubt that providence ordered that the Syrians heard the sound of an army coming and fled from the camp. If God plans something for you then it must come to pass. On Day 28, I want to conclude this story by talking to you a little more on God's Providence.

Testimony

I was working at a call centre and I was not comfortable in the job. It was paying but it was not conducive for me to work. I had to miss church very often due to the constant shift changes. I prayed and laid out my options. I made the decision to resign not knowing where the next job would come from. I resigned in June and in September when I thought I was not going to get a job, I got a call from a school to be a Guidance Counsellor for eight months. I worked alongside a wonderful woman of God known as Carlene Dacres and she encouraged me daily to do the will of the Lord. To date, we still correspond and she still serves as a counsellor. I thank God for that move because it aligned me with Carlene and changed my life entirely. The move you make might be your best move yet.

I beseech you therefore, brethren, by the mercies of God: Trust God with the moves you make.

Some decisions may seem stupid but pray about them, ask God for direction and trust Him with your moves.

Brawta Scripture

"Trust in the LORD with all your heart; do not depend on your own understanding" (Proverbs 3:5, NLT).

REFLECTION

What bold moves are you willing to make?

_____

_____

_____

_____

_____

_____

_____

Have you spoken to God about it?

_____

_____

_____

_____

_____

_____

Have you made the move already?

_____

_____

_____

_____

_____

_____

_____

If you have, has God given you consent?

_____

_____

_____

_____

_____

Let's talk to God about the moves we want to make in our lives today.

Write to God

_____

_____

_____

_____

Day 28

TRUST GOD'S PROVIDENCE

In completing our talk on the lepers in the book of 2 Kings, I want to encourage you to trust God's providence. The text below highlights Divine providence.

"For the Lord had caused the Aramean army to hear the clatter of speeding chariots and the galloping of horses and the sounds of a great army approaching" (2 Kings 7:6, NLT).

Encouragement

Providence declared that the lepers would survive. Providence is God's perfect plan coming into action. The universe works by the hand of God. Theories are evolving talking about the universe working in the favours of others. Or that karma is real. I want you to join me in throwing out that ridiculous idea. The universe cannot work in your favour unless God directs it. Divine providence declares that you'll survive what you are going through. You need to trust God's providence. Whatever is happening in your life, God has a hand in planning a route that will benefit you. Trusting God without knowing the next move is exciting. It is exhilarating. In this season, trust God's providence.

Testimony

My big brother in ministry, Minister Leroy Hutchinson was preaching at a crusade one night, and a young man by the name of Nigel Powell was present. His testimony was that he was a bad boy and was raised in a volatile area. He went to church and he heard a voice telling him to carry additional clothing. Little did he know that he was going to be baptized. The word that night hit him right in the heart and he was baptized immediately. Today, Nigel Powell works alongside Leroy and me with the company Operation Youth Reap. He serves the company as the Director for Mentorship. Divine providence declared that he would be saved on a specific day by the Word of God preached by a specific preacher. Thank you Jesus for Divine providence. May you trust the hand of God today.

I beseech you therefore, brethren, by the mercies of God: Trust God's providence.

Not everything will work out how you want it to but trust God that His plan will always work out for you. What you want may not be what is needed.

Brawta Scripture

"But he knows where I am going. And when he tests me, I will come out as pure as gold" (Job 23:10 NLT).

REFLECTION

Do you think God has your best interest at heart?

_____

_____

_____

_____

_____

_____

_____

Do you believe Providence is working in your favor?

_____

_____

_____

_____

_____

_____

_____

_____

_____

_____

I'll suggest the answer for you, Yes and Amen. Let's talk to God:

Write to God

_____

_____

_____

_____

_____

_____

_____

Day 29

YOU ARE ANOINTED

Today we are going to talk about being anointed for what is ahead. The text below shares the story of David being anointed, King.

So as David stood there among his brothers, Samuel took the flask of olive oil he had brought and anointed David with the oil. And the Spirit of the Lord came powerfully upon David from that day on. Then Samuel returned to Ramah (1 Samuel 16:13 NLT).

Encouragement

David was being trained in the backside of the desert. Little did he know that his training was preparing him for the office of King. He had to fight lions and bears to defend the sheep he was shepherding. Just like David, God has given us training in a specific area. You are anointed for the task ahead of you. You are designed for this. Just be warned that the anointing is going to cause persons to dislike you but that is all right. You are called for this.

Testimony

I was trained in 2017 with Heart Trust NTA to facilitate BPO training for persons to work in the Call Centre. My training was not put into effect until 2019, when the Ministry of Education, Youth and Information called me to be a Master Trainer. I was trained for that. I was anointed for it. I had the experience. You are anointed in this season for the task you have.

I beseech you therefore, brethren, by the mercies of God: Believe you are anointed.

Your anointing does not have to come with an office. God will prepare you to take on Goliaths and, in that season, you may not sit on a throne. Don't feel dismayed. David did it and later in life, he sat on the throne. You are anointed, work with it and complete your tasks.

Brawta Scripture

"You prepare a feast for me in the presence of my enemies. You honor me by anointing my head with oil. My cup overflows with blessings" (Psalms 23:5 NLT).

REFLECTION

What task are you currently working on?

_____

_____

_____

_____

_____

_____

Do you think you are anointed for it?

_____

_____

_____

_____

_____

_____

_____

_____

_____

_____

Let's talk to God.

Write to God

_____

_____

_____

_____

_____

_____

_____

_____

Day 30

YOUR HELP COMES FROM GOD

The text below tells us where our help comes from. Your help comes from God.

"I look up to the mountains— does my help come from there? My help comes from the Lord, who made heaven and earth!" (Psalms 121:1-2 NLT)

Encouragement

This Psalm is one birthed from the Psalmist when going to Palestine after the captivity. He assured himself that his coming help would not fail him. This is a very well-known Psalm and we can rest assured, like the Psalmist, that our help also comes from God. Sometimes it is in troubling situations we remember where our help comes from. The Psalmist is in Babylonian exile and far away from his hometown Jerusalem. Jerusalem has temples surrounded by mountains where the Lord would have met with Moses and the Lord's people. The mountain of which the Psalmist spoke was the mountain where Zion was built, and where the Lord promised to send help.

Sometimes we find ourselves in the position of the Psalmist and ask: "Where does my help come from?" We too, like the Psalmist, must be able to give an answer to our own question, "my help comes from God." The Psalmist assured himself that though he was still in exile, the God that he was serving would send help. And this help that comes from God will not fail. 30 Days have ended and I hope you have been powered up thus far. In our second volume of *Power Up*, we continue this interesting look at Psalm 121 and focus on God, THE KEEPER.

Testimony

I went for a job interview in Montego Bay in the year 2017. Heading home from the interview, the bus I was on was involved in an accident. The road was wet and the bus was speeding. It flipped three times and crashed into a light post with its wheels facing the sky. Checks revealed that 19 persons were injured and 1 person died. In the midst of the flipping, I held my head down and whispered, "help me, Lord." I came out with just a scrape and a Good Samaritan, a lady travelling with her children stopped and God sent them my way. She travelled from Trelawny all the way to Spanish Town, gave me J$2000 and dropped me at my grandmother. Praise the Lord Jesus, my help comes from God.

I beseech you therefore, brethren, by the mercies of God: Know where your help comes from.

Friends and family will fail you and may not give you the help you need, but rest assured that your help comes from Jehovah who made the heavens and the earth.

Brawta Scripture

"I took my troubles to the Lord; I cried out to him, and he answered my prayer" (Psalms 120:1 NLT).

REFLECTION

For what do you need help?

_____

_____

_____

_____

_____

_____

Have you been calling out to God?

_____

_____

_____

_____

_____

_____

_____

_____

_____

_____

_____

Let's talk to God about His divine help.

Write to God

_____

_____

_____

_____

_____

_____

_____

FINAL ENCOURAGEMENT

BE GREAT AND DO GREAT THINGS FOR GOD

The Lord directs the steps of the godly. He delights in every detail of their lives. Though they stumble, they will never fall, for the Lord holds them by the hand (Psalm 37:23-24, NLT).

Encouragement

Welcome to the final day of this encouragement guide. Today is simple. I just want to encourage you to be great. I coined the term: *Be Great and Do Great Things for God* as a mantra to guide my everyday life and activities. Every day I close my radio programme by encouraging the listeners to be great. I leave with you the closing words I use to end my on-air programmes.

You are here with a purpose so live your life on purpose. Be great and do great things for God.

Remember, greater is He that is in you than he that is in the world. It is a victory day and God has given you enough grace, mercy and strength to go through the day. Let no one steal your joy and let no one steal your thunder.

Today is your day to be the best you that God has called you to be. You may stumble but the great will never fall because the Lord directs your steps. God has you in the hollow of His hand and He has commanded you to be the best version of you. Today, you have completed 30 encouragements to help build your faith, trust and hope in God. Now, it is time for you to be great and do great things for God. You can do greater than what you are doing now and God expects you to step out into greatness. I encourage you today, be great and do great things for God.

Testimony

My mantra helps me every day of my life along with my closing words on air. I have a philosophy that I live by. I tell myself every day that whatever I do I must do it to the best of my ability. I had no training and experience in media but I ended up working in the field. Each time I turned on the microphone I was instantly touching lives. I used that great opportunity to make Christ known to the world.

I told the Lord in a sermon I preached that I want to do extraordinary things and now I see the extraordinary happening. The Greater One in me has awakened the greatness and today, I can say that I have been doing great things and greater is yet to come. I touch lives on a daily basis by just being me. Someone called me and shared with me that just hearing me talk about God had encouraged them to keep the faith. Whatever you are doing, be great at doing it and make sure it is pleasing to God.

I beseech you therefore, brethren, by the mercies of God: Be great and do great things.

Do not settle for ordinary events and ordinary life, push yourself to do great things. For the greater one is in you and therefore greater things shall you do. You are great. BE GREAT.

Brawta Scripture

"I tell you the truth, anyone who believes in me will do the same works I have done, and even greater works, because I am going to be with the Father" (John 14:12, NLT).

"But you belong to God, my dear children. You have already won a victory over those people because the Spirit who lives in you is greater than the spirit who lives in the world" (1st John 4:4, NLT).

REFLECTION

What mantra do you live by?

_____

_____

_____

_____

_____

What is your philosophy of life?

_____

_____

_____

_____

_____

_____

Do you believe you have what it takes to do great things for God?

_____

_____

_____

_____

_____

_____

Write to God

Create a mantra if you do not have one. Construct a philosophy to live by and finally write the miracles you wish to see done by the hands of God through you.

_____

_____

_____

_____

_____

PREPARATION

That's the whole story. Here now is my final conclusion: "Fear God and obey his commands, for this is everyone's duty" (Ecclesiastes 12:13, NLT).

My conclusion is as simple as that of Solomon. If you want to be strengthened along your Christian journey you must obey God. In order to build your faith, trust and hope in God read His word daily and live accordingly. If this book has inspired or motivated you to live for God more than ever please share it with someone. Here is my prayer for you.

My Prayer for You

Father, I come to you in the name of Jesus Christ our Lord and Savior. I present the reader before you. You know them by name and by nature. You are sovereign over their lives and you are the protector for the future days to come. I ask that you will strengthen them. Let their hope be built on the firm foundation of your word. Cause their faith in you to be unshaken. When the winds of life come blowing their way may their faith remain steadfast in you and let their trust be solid. I pray God that you will bless them in their going out and in their coming in.

I pray that they will walk into their rightful calling in your kingdom. Cause them to see miracles and may signs follow their life and ministry. I pray that their faith will not fail and that they will stand with you until the end. Touch them. Give them the inspiration to do what you have birthed in them to do. Father, they too have books to write, sermons to preach, lyrics to write, songs to sing, people to motivate, they do have great things that need to be done. Give them the push to get it done. Father, I come against procrastination and the spirit of doubt that would want to tell them that they cannot do it. I break that accursed cycle of incompletion from over their lives.

Father, they may have started out with great ideas but have failed to complete but let today be the day they find passion and drive to complete what they have started. I come against the enemy's tricks and schemes to devour them. Even as they read this prayer we nullify the plans of the enemy. We come against stagnation in the spirit realm and we pray that they will soar higher than they have ever been. Great One I pray that you will cause them to do great things for you, in Jesus name. Amen.

Pray with Me

Father, thank you for your many blessings bestowed upon me. Thank you for your gifts given to enhance my life. Thank you for the calling upon my life. Thank you for the purpose birthed within me. Thank you for the new mercies granted to me each morning. Thank you for your love towards me. Thank you for covering me, shielding me from the enemy and protecting me from me. Father, I pray in the name of Jesus that I shall not be less than what you have called me to be but I shall walk in a greater calling, greater anointing and into a greater relationship with you, in Jesus name. Amen.

UPCOMING BOOKS

Look out for ***Power Up, Volume 2*** with another 30 days of encouragement to build your faith, hope and trust in God. In addition to *Power Up, Volume 2*, get ready for ***Overcoming***. Overcoming personal struggles faced during life on earth is quite a task, but with God we can overcome all things. In this riveting discourse, the book ***Overcoming*** looks at certain issues that humans face in life and applies biblical principles in overcoming those issues. Not only is there Biblical foundation for overcoming certain issues but also psychological and sociological understanding will be applied to transform readers from being under the weather to overcoming the debris blown at them.

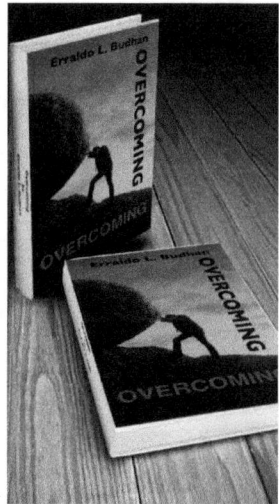

We will look at overcoming **FEAR**. Different aspects of fear will be highlighted and biblical remedies will be given to help us overcome. Also, overcoming what I consider to be the demon of **PROCRASTINATION**. Do you procrastinate often? Well, the Bible has an answer for everything and in *Overcoming* we will explore the biblical tenets of how we overcome procrastination and much more issues. Interesting reflections, transformational activities and more await you when you get the book: ***Overcoming.*** It is designed to assist you in transforming your life into the life God wants you to have.

> I have told you these things, so that in me you
> may have peace. In this world you will have
> trouble. But take heart! I have overcome the
> world (John 16:33, NIV).

ABOUT THE AUTHOR

L ay Minister Erraldo Budhan holds a Bachelor of Arts Degree in Theology from the Jamaica Theological Seminary and is currently enrolled at the Caribbean Graduate School of Theology where he is pursuing a Masters in Theological Studies. Erraldo has also completed a short study at the New Covenant Bible Institute where he is pursued two courses, one in History and Polity of the Church of God of Prophecy and another in Church Administration.

He has completed a Master Trainer workshop with the Ministry of Education Youth and Information where he has been certified to train persons in understanding the BPO industry and customer service. He is a trained Guidance Counsellor, a Radio Announcer with Love101 FM and a Job Coach with HEART NTA serving St. Catherine Jamaica.

He has been a Christian for the past 10 years and has no regrets of his decision to serve the Lord Jesus Christ. He currently worships at the Life Centre Tabernacle Church of God of Prophecy. He has been appointed to the office of Parish Youth and Young Adult Ministry Director for the Church of God of Prophecy St. Catherine East, and a Board Director with Operation Youth Reap Ltd. Erraldo also serves his church at the national level as a member of the National Convention Planning Committee and National Public Relations Committee of the Church of God of Prophecy Jamaica.

He strongly believes that the Lord has called him into an apostolic leadership and has confirmed such calling through numerous prophetic words. With such a calling on his life, his aim is to cultivate young leaders to develop their gifts and find their purpose in ministry.